"It's the Christmas holiday, and nothing
is going to ruin my day at the beach."

"Deck the hulls and bows with holly!"

"Fa-la-la-la-la-la — gulp!"

"I don't like any holiday where a guy in a red suit breaks into my house, and . . . SpongeBob, where are you?"

"Ahh, silent night."

"Snow will put Squidward in a jolly mood.
These stale Krabby Patty buns will make it a white Christmas."

"Do you know what gift would make me happy, SpongeBob?
Peace and quiet!"

"Help, SpongeBob! These lights have got me!"

"I'll make Squidward the most special holiday Krabby Patty ever. No one can escape its powerful goodness!"

"Special delivery!"

"If I take one bite, will you leave me alone?
It does kind of smell okay . . . and it looks . . . mmmm!"

"I can't lie, SpongeBob. This is pretty good."